THE
SURVIVAL KIT
FOR
YOUNG
BLACK MEN

THE SURVIVAL KIT FOR YOUNG BLACK MEN

"A Christian Guide to Manhood"

SHEILA CJ SOLOMON

Primix Publishing
11620 Wilshire Blvd
Suite 900, West Wilshire Center, Los Angeles, CA, 90025
www.primixpublishing.com
Phone: 1-800-538-5788

Published by Primix Publishing: 05/20/2024

ISBN: 979-8-89194-129-8(sc)
ISBN: 979-8-89194-228-8(hc)
ISBN: 979-8-89194-130-4(e)

Library of Congress Control Number: 2024905156

Any people depicted in stock imagery provided by iStock are models, and such images are being used for illustrative purposes only.

Certain stock imagery © iStock.

Because of the dynamic nature of the Internet, any web addresses or links contained in this book may have changed since publication and may no longer be valid. The views expressed in this work are solely those of the author and do not necessarily reflect the views of the publisher, and the publisher hereby disclaims any responsibility for them.

A SURVIVAL KIT FOR YOUNG BLACK MEN
"A CHRISTIAN GUIDE TO MANHOOD"

CONTENTS

INTRODUCTION

This book is named "The Survival Kit for Young Black Men, A Christian Guide to Manhood." It was divinely inspired and purposed to be shared with young black men as they enter manhood.

Do you realize that "you" are one of our most precious resources to obtaining our destiny? We need strong, educated, courageous, and fearless young leaders, as well as family men, to take our communities to the next level of our destiny as black people. However, we will never get there without you knowing and understanding what you are facing in the world, and more importantly what God wants and requires from your lives.

Knowledge is the most powerful tool that you can possession, because once you have it, no one can ever take it away from you. You can choose to use it to empower yourself and your community or you can choose not to use it at all, but you will always possess it.

The Word tells you that to have wisdom and understanding is far better than silver or gold (Proverbs 3-14). It also tells you that if you ask God for wisdom and understanding, He will gladly give it to you. (James 1-5).

This book will provide you with worldly knowledge and godly wisdom. Use it as a quick reference guide to God's word concerning his plan for your life in the areas of career, money management, giving, using your gifts and talents, love, marriage, stress and even racism. Take its wisdom, knowledge, and understanding as you enter manhood and make a difference with your life! It only takes a minute to read, but the blessings will continually overflow through out your lifetime.

Be Blessed,

Sheila CJ Solomon

YOU HAVE A CHOICE / KNOW THE FACTS

"… Choose for yourself this day whom you will serve …"
Joshua 24:15

Families: *Today Black Americans make up 13.5% of the US population: There are 8.5 million black family households (65%) 45% are married couples and 55% are single. In 1940 there were 77% married, 18% single women, and 5% single men. (US Census 2007)*

- In 2009, 67% of Black families headed by single women.
- In 2008, 72% of Black, 66% of Native American, 53% of Hispanics, 29% of Whites, and 17% of Asians children were born out of wedlock.
- In 2002, 63% to 35% decline in Black Marriage Rate from 1950.
- In 2007, 1.2 million grandparents live with their grandchildren 18 years and under: 50% are responsible for the care of these children.
- In 2005, 35% of all abortions were by Black women: 17.4% were 19 years and under.

Housing: *As of July 2007, US Census Bureau identified 40.7 million Black Americans: 55% reside in the South, 18% Northeast, 18% Midwest, 9% West vs. 77% in South in 1940. The top 5 cities with Black population are New York, Chicago, Detroit, Philadelphia, and Houston. The top 5 cities with Black migration are Atlanta, Dallas, Charlotte, and Orlando.*

- 52% live in cities.
- 36% live in suburbs.
- 12% live in rural areas
- 43% own their homes
- 80% of American's homeless are Black.

Education: *In 2004 there were 4.5 million Black American men between the ages of 15-29 living in the US, which represents about 14% of all men in this age group. (The Henry J Kaiser Family Foundation- Fact Sheet 2006)*

- In 2005, 77% of Blacks males graduated High School.
- In 2005, 7.5% of Black males attended college and graduated compared to 17% Whites, 35% Asians, and 5.9% Hispanics.
- 35% of Black Athletes in NCAA Division I schools graduate within six years.
- 75% of NCAA Division I Black Athletes fail to graduate.

Drugs & Crime: *Young Black Americans are disproportionately represented in the criminal justice system. The percentage of young Black Americans in prison is nearly three times that of Hispanics and seven times that of young White men. (The Henry J. Kaiser Family Foundation – Fact Sheet 2006) The" War on Crime" of the 1960s shifted from rehabilitation of offenders and job training to "do something about American's drug problem" and spending more money on building prisons. (FinalCall.comNews- 6/2010)*

- In 2003, the Justice Department reports incarceration rates has tripled for Black American and increased tenfold for Hispanics, from 1974-2001.
- By the end of 2001, about 16.6% of adult Black American males were currently or former inmates, compared to 7.7% of Hispanics, and 2.6% of White males.
- Arrests for drug violations skyrocketed from 1980-1993: White inmates increased 163% and Black inmates increased 217%.
- Black American males comprise about 14% of the population, 13% of drug users, 35% of all arrests for drug possession, 55% of all convictions and 74% of all those sentenced to prison for possession.
- By the end of 1993, ½ of all Federal and State prisons were Blacks American males.
- 1 of 3 Black American men between 20-29 is in prison, on probation, or on parole.
- In 1999 1.5 million Black American children in the U.S. had at least one parent in state or federal prison.
- In some states incarceration for drug related crimes causes the lost of voting rights, lost of access of public housing, lost of financial Aide to attend college, and even social services benefits.
- President Obama recently signed a bill that reduces minimum sentences for crack cocaine violations attempted to reduce the disparity between time served for crack and powder cocaine, the same drug that have deep racial implications.

Employment: *People with more education tend to have higher incomes, but in 2002 at every educational level, Black Americans with the same education made less than*

Whites. The unemployment rate for young Black American men is over twice the rate for young White, Hispanic, and Asian men. (The Henry J. Kaiser Family Foundation-Fact Sheet 2006)

- Black adult employments rates have remained twice as high as Whites for more than 30 years and three times as high among young people.
- Black men earn 67% of what White men earn.
- 21% of High School dropouts are unemployed.
- 53% of Black men 25-34 are unemployed or earn too little to support a family of four.
- 3.2 Black Lawyers
- 3% Black Doctors
- Less than 1% Black Architects.
- Blacks are twice as likely to work for city, state, or federal government.
- In the private sector, 1.9% hold critical positions in America's largest corporations like Merrill Lynch, American Express, AOL Time Warner, Citigroup, Verizon, United Parcel Service, General Electric, and Morgan Stanley to name a few.
- Black Business still caters to Black consumers in communications, and entertainment, while Black banks and Insurance companies decline.
- Black Entrepreneurship is on the rise, Blacks 24-35 are 50% more likely than Whites to participate in entrepreneurial activities, Russell Simmons, Sean Combs, Jay Z, and Tyler Perry to name a few.

Health: *The leading causes of death for all young men ages 15-29 regardless of race are unintentional injury (car accidents, firearm, or drowning), suicide, and homicide. For Black American males more deaths are caused by homicide than any other cause. (The Henry J. Kaiser Family Foundation-Fact Sheet 2006) In addition, HIV/AIDS is the sixth leading cause of death in young Black Americans aged 20-24(Center for DiseaseControl-2006).*

- In 2006, the CDC reports the top five leading cause of death for Black males aged 15-19 are: 1) Homicide-50.7%, 2) Unintentional Injury-25.3%, 3) Suicide-5.3%, 4) Cancer-2.9%, and 5) Heart Disease- 2.9%
- In 2010, the CDC reports Black Americans continue to have the highest rate of STDs (Sexually Transmitted Disease) than any other race/ethnicity in the US.
- In 2006, Black American males accounted for two-thirds of new HIV

infections (65%) among all Blacks: Black males were 6 times as high as White men, 3 times that of Hispanics, and twice that of black women.

- In 2006, 63% of new infections were from MSM (Men who have sex with men) among all black men. More new infections occurred among young black MSM (age 13-29) than among any other age and racial group of MSM.
- In a lack of awareness of HIV study among MSM in five cities, 67% of HIV infected black MSM were unaware of their infection.

YOUR SPIRITUALITY/ KNOW WHO YOU ARE!

"A Chosen Generation…" 1Peter 2:9

Royalty
"You are a chosen generation, royal priesthood, his own special people …"
1Peter 2:9

A Child of God
"Beloved now we are children of God, and it has not yet been revealed what we shall be, but we know that when He is revealed, we shall be like Him, for we shall see Him as He is." John 3:2

An Heir to the Kingdom
"And if children, then heirs, heirs of God and joint heir with Christ, if indeed we suffer with Him, that we may also be glorified together with Him." Romans 8: 17

Set Apart
"You have been set apart as holy to the Lord your God and He has chosen you to be His own special treasure from all the nations."
Deuteronomy 14:2

A Transformer
"And do not be conformed to this world, but be transformed by the renewing of your mind, that you may prove what is good and acceptable and the perfect will of God." Romans 12:12

Fearless
"For God has not given us the spirit of fear, but power and love and a sound mind." 2Timothy 1:7

An Over Comer

"Yet in all these things we are more than conquerors, through Him who loved us." Romans 8: 37

An Endurer

"... The race is not to the swift..." Ecclesiastes 9:11 "... but he who endures to the end will be saved." Matthew 10:22

The Tattoo

After 20 years of hearing mini sermons from his parents on how tattoos and ear piercing would not be allowed, while he was still living in his Christian parents' home, he made a decision to do the unthinkable. He got a tattoo!

You see, he was turning 21 next month and although he was still living with his parents, he was ready to make a statement about who he was. He graduated from high school and was in his junior year of college, he even had a part time job at Lowes. Next year he would graduate college with a business degree. He was a respectful son and he was on track with his parent's expectations and aspirations for his life. He also was a Christian. He gave his life to Christ when he was 10 years old, but he still decided to get a tattoo.

The tattoo was located on his upper left arm and stopped midway to his elbow. It was a scroll and written on it where these words, "You Are A Chosen Generation, A Royal Priesthood, HIS Special People!" When he revealed the tattoo to his parents, he didn't know how they were going to react. He was nervous and a little scared, but he was 21 years old and by law, his parents were no longer responsible for him. It was his statement about who he was and how he defined himself. He was on his way to becoming a self-sufficient man, so he stepped out on faith with this move. To his surprised they did not yell or scream or ask him to move out of their home.

His Dad's response was, "So you got yourself a tattoo, I guess you think you're a man now? Well at least you can wear a short sleeve shirt without seeing it." His Mom smiled and said, "Son, our job is done and I'm so proud that you really know who you are! Oh, by the way, please wait until to get your own apartment before you pierce you ears."

YOUR INTERGRITY, NOT YOUR "REP"

"Your reputation is what you do when people are looking; your integrity is what you do when no one is looking." Pastor Fred Davis

To Become a Man of Integrity you must Trust God, Give Freely, and Seek Wisdom (Proverbs 3:5-14)

- Trust in the Lord with all your heart and lean not on your own understanding. In all ways acknowledge Him and He will direct your paths.
- Do not be wise in your own eyes. Fear the Lord and Depart from evil. It will be health to your flesh and strength to your bones.
- Honor the Lord with your possessions and with the first fruits of all your increase. So, your barns will be filled with plenty, and your vats will overflow with new wine.
- My son do not despise the chastening of the Lord, Nor detest His Correction. For whom the Lord loves, He corrects. Just as a father, the son in whom he delights.
- Happy is a man who finds "Wisdom" and the man who gains understanding. For her proceeds are better than the profits of silver and her gain better than fine gold.

Be Consistence, Not Wishy-Washy (James 5:12)
- But above all, my brethren, do not swear either by heaven or by earth or with any other oath, but let your "Yes be Yes" and your "No, No", lest you fall into judgment.

Be True to God's Word (Galatians 6:6-8)
- Let him who is taught the word; share in all good things with him who teaches. Do not be deceived; God is not mocked for whatever a man sows, that he will reap.

Live by "The Fruits of the Spirit" (Galatians 5:27)
- But the fruits of the spirit are love, joy, peace, longsuffering, kindness, goodness, faithfulness, gentleness, and **self control** against such there is no law.

INTEGRITY

I – Inspired by God

N – Need for Truth
T - To "Your Self" Be True

E - Excited about You

G - God's Plan for You

R - Responsible Lifestyle

I - Intelligent Decisions

T - Tough Mentally

Y – Your Word Is Bond

REPUTATION

R - Represents Other's Thoughts

E - Easy to Impress

P - People Pleasing

U - Unsure of Yourself

T - Terrified of Rejection

A - Afraid of Failure

T - Trauma and Drama

I - Insecure Self Image

O - Overrated

N – Needs Approval of Others

It's your integrity that will lead you successfully through life. If you know who you are and to whom you belong to, there is nothing you cannot accomplish in this life. God has given you power through Christ, to do all things. You need only to dream it, believe it can be done, and receive it will be done, through activating your faith. Develop a relationship Him and you will tap into your integrity. Say what you mean, and mean what you say, even when no one is looking.

Your reputation "rep" is often short lived and can lead you to places you never want to go. Reputation is overrated by the young and especially young men. It stems from being unsure and uncertain of whom you really are. Your desire to be poplar and accepted by a particular group takes priority in your life. However, the older and more mature you become, the less you are concerned about what other people think of you and fitting into the crowd. You realize your true friends are the ones that accept you for what's in your heart, and not what you're wearing!

YOUR FINANCES/YOUR MONEY

"And to one He gave five talents, to another two, and to another one. Each according to his own ability." Matthew 25:15

Manage your money to make a profit (Matthew 25:27-28)

"You ought to have deposited my money with the bankers, and at my coming I would have received back my own with interest. So, take the talent from him and give it to him who has ten talents."

Give God the Tithe, So you will be blessed (Malachi 3:8-11)

"Bring the tithes into the storehouse that there may be food in my house. And try Me now, in this says the Lord of hosts. If I will not open for you the windows of heaven and pour out such a blessing that there will not be room enough to receive it."

Give Generously, So God Gives Generously to You (Luke 6:28)

"Give and it will be given to you; a Good measure, pressed down, shaken together and running over, it will be poured into your lap. For with the same measure you use, it will be measured to YOU."

Money Matters

Jesus' ministry lasted 3 years, it began in Nazareth and ended in Jerusalem. The two most discussed topics were "money" and "hell." Therefore, money matters to God and money mattered to Christ. Jesus came into the word to give instructions on how to properly manage our money. What an awesome revelation!

Everyone quotes Jesus on these scriptures, "The love of money is the root of all evil." 1Timothy 6:10 and "It is easier for a camel to go through the eye of a needle than a rich man to enter heaven." Luke 18:25, as God's view towards money.

However, it's not the money that is evil, rather it's the "love" of money that corrupts the human spirit. It's not that a rich man cannot get into heaven, rather it's when the man becomes rich, he often forgets, if it was not for God being the provider, there would be no rich man. God is the ultimate provider of everything we have or can do. In terms of money, He never wants us to not get it twisted. When you have money or wealth it's because God gave you the ability to acquire it. He also wants us to love Him more! No one or nothing can come before our love for him, especially not money.

Let me also dispel the myth that you must be poor to truly serve God. No, that is not God's plan for your life. God does not want you to be poor, rather He wants you to continually grow in wealth and wisdom. Each of us is given talents according to our own ability. I'm sorry but, we all do not start at the same place in life. However, He requires each to manage what he gives us well. If we manage well then, He gives us the ability to have more and to continually grow in wealth. This is God's plan for your life.

Let me end the money matter with this biblical principal, "You Must Give To Receive." You must give the tithe to God first and He will give you a financial blessing greater than you can ever image. So many of us live our lives, with so little because we fail to activate the tithing principal. Then you must give to the less fortunate, you must give of your gifts and talents, and you must give praise and worship to your God. You must give to receive what God has in store for your life!

FINDING YOUR CAREER

*"Look for your God given gift and your gift will
make room for you." Bishop T.D. Jakes*

Know God's Intention for Your Life
"For I know the plans I have for you, says the Lord, plans of peace and not evil, to give you a future and hope..." Jeremiah 29:11

Seek God's Spiritual Gift Given When You Were Saved. Use Them to Serve Others and Edify The Church.
"Every good gift and perfect gift is from above and comes down from the Father of lights ..." James 1:17

"Having the gifts according to the grace that is given us, let us use them; if prophecy, let us prophecy in portion to our faith, or ministry, let us use it in ministering, he who teaches, in teaching, he who exhorts, in exhortation, he who gives, with liberality; he who leads, with diligence, he who shows mercy, with cheerfulness." Romans 12:6

Understand God Has No Limitation On What You Become
"For with God nothing is impossible." Luke 1:37

"I can do all things through CHRIST who strengthens me." Philippians 4:13

Embrace Your Faith
"But without faith it is impossible to please Him, for he who comes to God must believe that He is, and that He is the rewarder of those who diligently seek Him." Hebrews 11:6

"Now faith is the substance of things hoped for and the evidence of things not seen." Hebrews 11:1

FINDING YOUR WOMAN

"Let each man have his own wife and let each woman have her own husband. Let the husband render his wife affection due her and likewise also the wife to her husband." 1Corinthians 7:2-3

Realize What Is Acceptable in God's Eyes

"Marriage is honorable among all, and the bed undefiled, but fornicators and adulterers God will judge." Hebrews 13:4

"But I say to the unmarried and to the widows. It is good for them to remain as I am, but if they cannot exercise self control, let them marry. For it is better to marry than to burn with passion." 1Corinthians 7:8-9

"Flee sexual immorality... he who commits sexual immorality sins against his own body. Or do you not know that your body is a temple of the Holy Spirit who is in you, whom you have from God, and you are not your own? You were bought at a price; therefore, glorify God in your body and your spirit, which belongs to God." 1 Corinthian 6:18-20

Be Selective When Choosing Your Woman

"Deliver you from the immoral woman, from seductress who flatters with her words. Who forsake the companion of her youth and forgets the covenant of her God. For her house leads down to death and her paths to the dead." Proverbs 2:16-18

"Charm is deceitful, and beauty is passing, but a woman who fears the Lord, she shall be praised. Give her the fruit of her hands and let her own works praise her in her gates." Proverbs 31:30

Baby Mama / Baby Daddy Too Much Drama!

He's my baby daddy. She's my baby mama; these are common terms we use nowadays to describe parents of unwed children. Once upon a time, if a child was born out of wedlock the young woman felt a sense of shame and embarrassment. The young man felt a sense of guilt and obligation to marry and/ or provide for the child. The child was called illegitimate and even a bastard when folks got ugly. Thank God we have gotten away from such unhealthy language and stigmas, especially for the innocent baby boy or girl born into that lifestyle.

However, today, we can all agree that we have far too many baby mama, and baby daddy relationships. These high drama relationships produce unhealthy self images for mother, father, and the child. So often, we see the negativity spilling over into every area of everyday life. High School graduation rate is down; the Drop-out rate is up. College attendance is too low, and Incarceration is too high. Employment rates are down, and unemployment is way up. Child support and visitation rights, child abuse and neglect are at all time highs. Drama, drama, drama, too much drama!

Therefore, we can also agree this is not God's design for His family. Marriage is honorable to God. His family produces husbands, wives, and children, all living together. Granted all His families are not made of children conceived by both parents, but the children are parented by a union with a husband and a wife being led by God. His families include blended families with stepparents, adopted parents, stepchildren, foster children, and adopted children. Both husband and wife take on the full responsibility to raise their children to become the best they can be under the guidance and direction of God and His holy word. This is his design for His family!

When choosing your woman be selective, beauty is only skin deep! Over time gravity breaks the body down. What once was tight and right, now becomes not so tight and not so right. However, a beautiful woman at age 20 will remain a beautiful woman to you at age 70, if she has inner beauty. It's the inner beauty of woman that remains timeless. When searching for your dream woman, try to find a beautiful woman (inside & outside) who knows the Lord. Find a woman who's in relationship with God before she's in a relationship with you. If you can find that combination, your life will be blessed beyond measure. Find a Wife, Not A Baby Mama!

COPING WITH AUTHORITIES & RACISM

"Give to Cesar what belongs to him. But everything that belongs to God must be given to God," Matthew 22:21

Respect & Yield Those Who Have Authority Over You The Government, Police, Employers

"Therefore, submit yourself to every ordinance of man for the Lord's sake, whether to the king supreme, or to the governors as those who are sent by him for the punishment of evildoers and for the praise of those who do good. For this is the will of God, that by doing good you may put to silence the ignorance of the foolish men." 1Peter 2:13-15.

"For what credit is it if when you are beaten for your faults, you take it patiently? But when you do good and suffer, if you take it patiently, this is commendable before God. For this you were called, because Christ also suffered for us, leaving us an example, that you should follow His steps." 1Peter 2:20-21

Obey Parents and Pastors Authority

"Obey those who take rule over you and be submissive for they watch out for your soul, as those who must give an account. Let them do so with joy and not with grief for that would be unprofitable for you." Hebrews 13:17

Racism & Injustice Are Apart of This World … But God!

"Bond servant, obey in all things … and whatever you do, do it heartily as to the Lord and not to men." Colossians 3: 22

"But we also glory in tribulation, knowing that tribulations produce perseverance, and perseverance character and character hope. Romans 5:3

Do Not Become Bitter, Forgive & Become Better

"Pursue peace with all people and holiness with out which no one will see the Lord. Lest any root of bitterness springs up cause trouble and by this many become defiled." Hebrews 12:14-15

"If we live in the Spirit, let us also walk in the Spirit. Let us not become conceited, provoking one another, envying one another. Galatians 5:25-26

"And yet I show you a more excellent way... Love suffers long and is kind; love does not envy; love does not seek its own; is not provoked, thinks no evil; does not rejoice in iniquity, but rejoices in truth; bears all things, believes all things, hopes all things, endures all things, Love never fails." 1Corinthians 12:30 & 13:4-9

"You have heard that it was said, "You shall love your neighbor and hate your enemy." But I say to you, love your enemies, bless those who curse you, do good to those who hate you and pray for those who spitefully use you and persecute you, that you maybe sons of your Father in Heaven." Matthew 5:43-45

"For if you forgive men their trespasses, your heavenly Father will also forgive you. But if you don not forgive men their trespasses, neither will your Father forgive your trespasses." Matthew 6:14

COPING WITH THE STRESS OF IT ALL

"In this world you will have tribulations, but be of good cheer, I overcame the world." John 16:33

PRAY...Get A Personal Relationship With God!

"Be anxious for nothing, but in everything by prayer and supplication, with thanksgiving, let your requests be made to God and the peace of God, which surpasses all understanding, will guard your heart and mind through Christ Jesus." Philippians 4:6

"Rejoice always, pray without ceasing, in everything give thanks, for this is the will of God in Christ Jesus for you." Thessalonians 5:17

"Give ear to my works O Lord. Consider my mediation. Give heed to the voice of my cry. My King and my God, for to you I will pray. My voice you shall hear in the morning, O Lord. In the morning, I will direct it to you and I will look up." Psalm 5:1-3

God Has Your Back!

"As we know that all things work together for good to those who love God and those who are called according to His Purpose ... Moreover, whom He predestined, these He also called; whom He called these He also justified and when He justified these He also glorified." Romans 8:28 & 30

"And let us not grow weary while doing Good, for in due season, we shall reap, if we do not lose heart." Galatians 6:9

"For the battle is the Lord's and He will give you into our hands." 1Samules 17:47

THE ALPHA & OMEGA

PSALMS 27:1-5

- The Lord is my light and my salvation, whom shall, I fear?   The Lord is the strength of my life; of whom shall I be afraid?

- When the wicked came against me, to eat up my flesh, my enemies and foes, they stumbled and fell.

- Though an army may encamp against me. My heart shall not fear, though war may rise against me. In this I will be confident,

- One thing I have desired of the Lord that I will seek: that I will dwell in the house of the Lord all the days of my life, to behold the beauty of the Lord and inquire in His temple.

- For in the times of trouble. He shall hide me in His pavilion; in a secret place of His tabernacle; **HE SHALL HIDE ME...**

Amen

Each Day of Your Life

Choose Love

No occasion justifies hatred; no injustice warrants bitterness, choose love. Today you will love god and what God loves.

Choose Joy

You will invite your God to be the God of circumstance. You will refuse the temptation to be cynical... the tool of the lazy thinker. You will refuse to see people as anything less than human beings created by God. You will refuse to see any problem as anything less than an opportunity to see God.

Choose Peace

You will live forgiven. You will forgive so that you may live.

Choose Patience

You will overlook the inconveniences of the world. Instead of cursing the one who takes your place, you'll invite him to do so. Rather than complain that the wait is too long, you thank God for a moment to pray. Instead of clinching your fist at new assignments, you will face them with joy and courage.

Choose Kindness

You will be kind to the poor, for they are alone. Kind to the rich for they are afraid. And kind to the unkind for such is how God has treated you.

Choose Goodness

You will go without a dollar before you take a dishonest one. You will be overlooked before you boast. You will confess before you accuse. You choose goodness.

Choose Faithfulness

Today you will keep your promises. Your debtors will not regret their trust. Your friends will not question your word. Your children will never question or fear your love.

Choose Gentleness

Nothing is won by force. You choose to be gentle. If you raise your voice, may it be only in praise. If you clench your fist, may it only be in prayer. If you make a demand, may it only be of yourself.

Choose Self-Control

You are a spiritual being...You will be drunk only by joy. You will be impassioned only by faith. You will be influenced only my God. You will be taught only by Christ. You choose self-control.

Love, joy, peace, kindness, goodness, faithfulness, gentleness, and selfcontrol, the fruit of the spirit...to these you commit your day. If you succeed, you will give thanks. If you fail, you will seek God's grace. And when the day is done, you will place you head on your pillow and rest.

Max Lucado / When Gods Whispers Your Name

Statistical References Listed in "Know The Facts"

1. *The Black Condition, The American Directory of Certified Uncle Toms, Chicago: Lushens, 2002*

2. *On Campus, Grin Statistics for African American Men, Bill Maxell, Times Staff Writer, 1/4/04.*

3. *The Rise of the Black Middle Class, Robert I. Harris Jr. Worldandi. com, February 1999, Volume 14*

4. *The Rise of the Black Entrepreneur: A New Force for Economics and Moral Leadership, Anthony B. Bradley, Research Fellow, Action Institute for the Study of Religion and Liberty, May 7, 2003*

5. *The Racial Income Gap, Two Nations, Andrew Hacker, Pipeline.com*

6. *Leading Causes of Death by Age Group, All Races, Male, United States, 2002, (HHS, CDC, NCHS)*

7. *Fact Sheet- HIV/AIDS Among African Americans, CDC-NCHSTP-Division of HIV/AIDS, 2003*

Additional Readings

1. *Why? Because You're Anointed T.D. Jakes*
2. *Rich Dad, Poor Dad, Robert T. Kiyosaki*
3. *Maximize The Moment, God's Action Plan for Your Life, T.D. Jakes*
4. *We Need the Men to Come Back, Kia Gregory, Philadelphia Weekly*
5. *Serious Business, New Start- Community Regeneration Online, Graham Readfern, Cover Story, 1/17/03.*